MW01000987

S THE LOST
SHEPHERD

Other Discovery House Publishers books by Warren W. Wiersbe

Bless You: Receiving and Sharing the Blessings of the Lord

Heirs of the King: Living the Beatitudes

Who Am I?: New Testament Pictures of the Christian Life

THE LOST SHEPHERD

FINDING AND KEEPING THE RIGHT PASTOR

ROBERT K. SPRADLING
WARREN W. WIERSBE

ILLUSTRATIONS BY RON WHEELER

Discovery House Publishers

Books, music, and videos that feed the soul with the Word of God

Box 3566 Grand Rapids, MI 49501

Discovery House Publishers is affiliated with RBC Ministries, Grand Rapids, Michigan.

Discovery House Books are distributed to the trade exclusively by Barbour Publishing, Inc., Uhrichsville, Ohio.

Requests for permission to quote from this book should be directed to: Permissions Department, Discovery House Publishers, P.O. Box 3566, Grand Rapids, MI 49501.

Unless otherwise indicated, Scripture quotations are from the *Holy Bible, New International Version®. NIV®.* Copyright © 1973, 1978, 1984 by International Bible Society. Used by permission of Zondervan. All rights reserved.

Library of Congress Cataloging-in-Publication Data
Spradling, Robert K.
The lost shepherd : finding and keeping the right pastor / Robert K. Spradling and Warren W. Wiersbe.
     p.   cm.
ISBN 978-1-57293-236-4
1. Clergy—Appointment, call, and election. 2. Vocation, Ecclesiastical. 3. Pastoral search committees. I. Wiersbe, Warren W. II. Title.
BV664.S67   2008   254—dc   222008000464

Interior design by Nicholas Richardson

Printed in Canada

08 09 10 11 12 / TP / 10 9 8 7 6 5 4 3 2 1

Contents

Preface

Our gracious God specializes in finding things. He found Adam and Eve when they were hiding among the trees of the garden (Genesis 3), and He sent His beloved Son "to seek and to save what was lost" (Luke 19:10). He helped Abraham's servant find a wife for Isaac (Genesis 24). When the enemy overwhelmed Israel, God found two courageous women named Deborah and Jael, and they delivered the nation (Judges 4–5). He helped Samuel find David and anoint him king of Israel (1 Samuel 16). When Barnabas went to Tarsus to locate his friend Saul (Paul), the Lord helped him and brought them both to minister to the church in Antioch (Acts 11:25–26).

God is never at a loss to find the right person for the task, and He will help you find the right pastor for your church. That's what this book is about. We want to give you spiritual guidance from the Bible in finding, calling, and keeping the right pastor.

Please keep your Bible at hand as you read, look up every reference, and read the verses to see how God's truth applies to the subject at hand. This book is not a substitute for your Bible. The search before you requires organization and administration, but most of all, it requires illumination from God's Word and God's Spirit.

There are no shortcuts in the spiritual adventure you are about to undertake, so learn to wait on the Lord. He will not fail you.

Robert K. Spradling and Warren W. Wiersbe

chapter 1

The Committee

DEFINITIONS OF A COMMITTEE:

A mutual protection society formed to guarantee that no one person can be held to blame for a botched . . . job that one man could have performed satisfactorily.

—Russell Baker

A group of the unfit, appointed by the unwilling, to do the unnecessary.

—Henry Cooke

A group of people who individually can do nothing and collectively decide that nothing can be done.

—Anonymous

We may smile or even laugh at these definitions of what a committee is and does, but as Christians, we reject every one of them. Why? Not because no committees fit these descriptions, but because these statements discredit the work of dedicated people seeking to accomplish God's will in this needy world. Many committees succeed, and some committees fail. If a committee does fail, it isn't simply because it is a committee but because the people involved didn't know how to do their job right (or perhaps somebody made it difficult for them to do it right). No matter what an organization is trying to accomplish, *everything rises or falls with leadership.* One of the purposes of this book is to help guide and encourage committee members like you, who have been placed in the position of leadership, in helping a congregation find and keep the right pastor.

Search the New Testament carefully, and you will find no mention of a Pastoral Search Committee (hereafter known as PSC). In the early years of the church, such committees were not needed because local church leaders were selected from the congregations. The apostles or their representatives chose qualified people in each church—believers who had been tested and proved—and they were set apart to lead the congregations serving Christ (Acts 6:1–7; 14:23; Titus 1:5). Those who shepherded the flock were known as "pastors and teachers" (Ephesians 4:11), as well as elders and overseers, or bishops (Acts 20:17, 28; 1 Peter 5:1–4).

But the church today has no apostles, although some denominations have bishops or superintendents who seek to minister in the apostolic tradition. However, it isn't unusual these days for members of a church ministry staff to be called from within their own congregation.[1] In fact, the new senior minister may have been trained by the congregation's previous pastor and prepared by him for the ministry. But most churches call the senior pastor from another church or a para-church ministry. That being the case, somebody has to find him, and that's where the PSC comes in.

---

1. This has both advantages and disadvantages. The advantages are that the church knows the worker and the worker knows the church, because he or she is already on the field and "knows the ropes." The disadvantage is the danger of "organizational inbreeding" so that nobody comes in with new ideas or a fresh view of the situation.

Great moments in church history: the first pastoral
search committee is formed.

A STATEMENT OF PURPOSE FOR THE PSC:

The task of the Pastoral Search Committee is to serve the Lord and the church by assisting the congregation in finding, calling, and keeping the right pastor, the one God has prepared for the church at this particular time in its ministry.

Pastor Leith Anderson makes this astute statement in his book *Dying for Change:* "Search Committees are too often chosen to be representative rather than competent." People should not be put on the PSC just to make sure the Funeral Lunch Committee gets a new kitchen, the teenagers a bigger gym, the choir a nicer robing room, and the Finance Committee a balanced budget. These are all excellent goals, but if the new pastor has any wisdom at all, he will first get acquainted with the congregation and then set his ministry priorities. And any PSC member who lobbies with a candidate in advance about these things ought to be rebuked.

A representative committee is frequently too large, and this makes it difficult for the group to get together. The committee needs quality, and not quantity. Moses sent twelve representative men to search Canaan, and ten men caused the whole enterprise to fail (Numbers 12–13). Joshua sent two men in and succeeded in taking the land (Joshua 2). Quality people will seek the mind of the Lord and look beyond their personal likes and dislikes. Five or seven of them are worth scores of immature but sincere Christians who have never served on an important committee. A PSC is not the place to start training young believers.

If possible, at least one of the committee members should be free to meet guest speakers or candidates at the airport, or, if they drive, to welcome them when they arrive in town. A husband and wife should do this together; it's unwise for the wives of committee members to provide this ministry. A husband and wife are best for the task. The church should pay whatever expenses the committee member incurs (such as mileage, parking, and meals).

Finally, the committee should be dedicated publicly at a morning service, and the congregation should be urged to pray daily for them. Perhaps a brief summary of what the committee is supposed to do would help prevent the interference of well-meaning church members who try to micromanage the work of the committee.

Here is a Statement of Faith to which all PSC members should subscribe. It should be modified to fit whatever local church distinctive must be considered.

A STATEMENT OF FAITH FOR THE PSC

1. We believe that Christ is the head of the church and will provide a pastor for our congregation if we submit to His will, pray, search the Word, and wait upon Him (Jeremiah 3:15; Luke 10:2; Philippians 4:19). Our task is not to please everybody in the church but to please the Lord.
2. We believe that the Lord will work in us and through us (Philippians 2:12–13) as we worship Him, maintain unity, and gather information about our church and the potential candidates He brings to us. Through this process, we believe the Lord will teach His church and prepare us to serve with our new shepherd.
3. We believe that it is our responsibility to "[speak] the truth in love" (Ephesians 4:15) and avoid all hypocrisy and deception. This means that we will keep confidence with our fellow PSC members and that the whole committee will communicate with the whole church at regular times.

4. We believe that the Spirit will be grieved if individual PSC members have "hidden agendas" and fail to practice Philippians 2:1–11. If we find ourselves seriously disagreeing and moving toward conflict, we promise to stop, examine our hearts in the light of the Word, pray, and take whatever steps are necessary to restore unity.

5. We believe that our work as a committee is a spiritual ministry, not simply an organizational responsibility, and that all that we do must honor and glorify the Lord (1 Corinthians 10:31).

6. We believe that God can use our individual skills and Christian experience to help direct us, and that in diversity there can be unity; but we will not depend only on ourselves but on Him (Proverbs 3:5–6). We will come to all meetings spiritually prepared, bring our Bibles with us, and take time at each meeting to pray for God's guidance and blessing.

THE PSC CHAIRPERSON

As we have already said, everything rises and falls with leadership. It's important that the members of the PSC and their chairperson be among the very best that the church has to offer to the Lord. The apostle Paul chided the Corinthian church because they appointed as leaders people who were "least esteemed in the church" (1 Corinthians 6:4 KJV). The NIV translates it "men of little account." We may not want to admit it, but not many people in the average church are qualified to chair so important a committee as the PSC. Whether the church, the elders, or the PSC chooses the chairperson itself, everyone should know the characteristics of an effective chairperson.

- Evident spiritual maturity and godliness and the ability to use the Scriptures in a practical way.
- Knowledge of the church—its background, people, problems, opportunities, and congregational dynamics.
- Skill in leading meetings. This means the ability to listen, to respond graciously in disagreements, and to anticipate what committee members may think or say. The chairperson must also possess that gentle strength that keeps the meeting on track and keeps people who want to dominate the discussion or go on time-wasting detours in line.
- An ability to enlist and encourage others (Acts 9:26–28; 11:19–30) as a "Barnabas" kind of person (Acts 11:24) who is willing to sacrifice (Acts 4:36–37).

No one person may have all of these qualities, but we ought to weigh the factors and make the very best choice. Of course the chairperson can't do the job alone but needs the prayer, counsel, and encouragement of the people on the committee as well as the people of the congregation. We must assist our leaders in dealing with problems or problem people (they usually go together) who are making the task more difficult than it ought to be. Here are some dangerous people to keep off of committees:

- People who interrupt others, try to dominate the discussion, and take nobody's ideas seriously but their own. They carry on private conversations or shuffle papers while others are speaking.
- People who are in a hurry to "get it over with," who try to "railroad" things through without allowing time for prayer, full discussion, and closure.
- People who go on "discussion detours" and especially like to talk about the "good old days." The past should be a rudder to guide us—not an anchor to hold us back.

Your job is to give your report. My job is to glance at my watch every few minutes to make sure you hurry up about it.

- People who resist new ideas and approaches to getting the work done.
- People who come to meetings unprepared and must always be brought "up to speed." They enjoy the special attention that they get, but their selfishness wastes precious hours of time.
- People who create tension when they are present and are not really missed when they are absent. Things seem to go better when they are gone.

Please don't be guilty of any of these offenses, and please help your chairperson eliminate them. *The process of calling a pastor does not necessarily create problems—it reveals them.* These problems may have been in the church family for years. A faithful committee is not afraid to deal with them and to help solve them.

THE PSC AND THE CHURCH OFFICERS

Keep in mind that the PSC is a temporary advisory committee and not a permanent administrative board. In doing your work, you don't take over the ministry of any officer or board that has been established by the congregation. It is also important to remember that the PSC must not operate in isolation but should cooperate with the key ministry people in the church (elders, deacons, and staff personnel) and keep them and the church family informed. Helping to bring about an orderly transition is one of the major tasks of your committee, and regular communication is one of the keys. Your chairperson is the logical one to serve as liaison with the church leaders, especially the official governing board, which should receive copies of the minutes of the PSC meetings. Of course, they keep the minutes confidential.

This official teamwork is essential when the time comes to invite a potential candidate to get acquainted with the church. It becomes especially important if the PSC recommends that the guest preacher become an official candidate and return to preach, ask questions, and be interviewed in depth. There must be people responsible for transportation, hospitality, scheduling and supervising interviews, showing the candidate family the community, and a host of other activities, not the least of which is giving the candidate and his family time to rest. (The tour of the community could wait until after the candidate has been officially called. It depends on how far away the family lives.)

We recommend that the leaders of the church and the PSC meet regularly for prayer and that the congregation frequently be urged to pray for God's direction in the calling of a new pastor. Certainly the matter should be mentioned each week in the Sunday morning pulpit prayer. One of the PSC members could be put in charge of this prayer emphasis. We also recommend that the official board call occasional congregational meetings for sharing information and prayer requests and to allow the church family to ask questions and voice concerns. It's amazing how many rumors and half-truths circulate while a church is searching for a shepherd, and dealing with them in a congregational meeting is better than discussing them with people individually.

We further suggest that both the committee and the church family read frequently the following Scriptures: John 10:1–18; Acts 20:17–38; 1 Timothy 3; Titus 1; and Ezekiel 34. (The shepherds Ezekiel wrote about were actually civil rulers in Judah, but the truths expressed apply to today's spiritual leaders as well.) They help us get God's outlook on what shepherding is all about. The better acquainted you are with what God says in His Word, the better equipped you will be to make the right decisions.

Your goals?

1. Finding a pastor who can sincerely say, "I know that when I come to you, I will come in the full measure of the blessing of Christ" (Romans 15:29).

I don't think there is much chance anyone is going to forget to pray for our pastor search process.

2. Helping to prepare a congregation that can say, "Now we are all here in the presence of God to listen to everything the Lord has commanded you to tell us" (Acts 10:33).

Sounds like a good combination!

chapter 2

The Congregation

There is no monument dedicated to the memory of a committee.

—Lester J. Pourciau

I've searched all the parks in all the cities and found no statues of committees.

—G. K. Chesterton

And whatever you do, whether in word or deed, do it all in the name of the Lord Jesus, giving thanks to God the Father through him.

—Colossians 3:17

You and your fellow committee members are the servants of the congregation, and your insignia of office is a towel, not a scepter (John 13:1–17). Don't expect to get reserved spaces in the church parking lot. You may have to endure the pains of criticism and misunderstanding and the hurts caused by rumors and misinformation, false accusations, and other forms of not-so-spiritual conduct. But keep Colossians 3:23–24 in mind—"Whatever you do, work at it with all your heart, as working for the Lord, not for men, since you know that you will receive an inheritance from the Lord as a reward. It is the Lord Christ you are serving." We serve a wonderful Master!

Never lose your sense of wonder at the miracle of the church. According to Acts 20:28, it is the "church of God," not *our* church, and the Lord has put His name on it. Paul was addressing the leaders of a local church and reminding them that Jesus died for the church and that the Holy Spirit was given to help the church select leaders who will do God's will. *We must be careful how we treat the local church.* "Don't you know that you yourselves are God's temple and that God's Spirit lives in you? If anyone destroys God's temple, God will destroy him; for God's temple is sacred, and you are that temple" (1 Corinthians 3:16–17).

Just as every family has a "secret script," with each family member playing his or her own role in order to keep the skeletons in the closet, so church families have scripts with all sorts of "characters" doing their bit. Here are some of them:

- The self-appointed resident theologians, who expect all matters to be brought under their omniscient scrutiny, because they are never wrong.
- The legalists, who study the church constitution as much as they study the Bible. They want to be sure the committee obeys the law of the Medes and Persians.
- The "listening post" people whose sponge-like ears soak up information and misinformation, but these people sometimes have a problem distinguishing the one from the other.
- The dedicated doubters whose pessimistic outlook on all matters drops a pall over business meetings and conversations. "We tried that once, and it didn't work," is their chief response. "There just aren't any good ministers left any more!" is another.
- The consecrated comedians who greet every problem with a laugh and try to solve difficulties with jokes. If the legalist comes to church wearing a suit of armor, the comedian wears a clown costume. A sense of humor is certainly important as

we seek to live and work together. Laughter can relieve tension and help us regain our perspective, and blessed is that person who knows when laughter is appropriate. But while laughter may help lubricate the machinery, it doesn't put fuel in the tank or guarantee that the compass is accurate.

- The denial experts, who try to make embarrassing problems disappear just by saying "Oh, that's over and settled!" or "Nobody worries about that any more!" or "What difference does it make?" Closing our eyes doesn't make things go away. It often only makes them worse.

Patiently listen to these people, learn what you can from them, make no promises—after all, the committee makes decisions together—and pray for them. God commands us to "accept one another" (Romans 15:1–7), and you never know how the Lord may use some of these saints in spite of their eccentricities.

As we noted earlier, the process of searching for a pastor doesn't *create* problems in your church—*it reveals them.* Like a sickness lurking in the body, the symptoms don't show up until the situation is just right. When there's no shepherd overseeing the flock, some of the sheep may become nervous and frightened and unwittingly start to create problems. Furthermore, the enemy knows the situation better than we do and might try to use a church officer with an inflated ego to create dissension and division. (Take time to read about Diotrephes—3 John 9–10.)

Sometimes it's wise for the church to call an interim pastor to preach (when there isn't a potential candidate in the pulpit) and to assist with the general pastoral work. If the official board and congregation agree to this, the availability of an experienced shepherd should take some of the pressure off both the board and the PSC. Set a specific time limit for the interim ministry—it can be renewed if necessary—*and make it clear that an interim pastor is not a candidate for the pulpit.*

I think you'll find our flock to be a pretty
typical congregation.

TAKING INVENTORY

"Be sure you know the condition of your flocks," King Solomon admonished the shepherds (Proverbs 27:23), and wise counsel it was for them in their day and is for us today. If the PSC is to do its work with integrity and unity, you must seek honest answers to these questions.

1. Why did our former pastor resign?
2. What part did the congregation play in the matter? The leaders?
3. Is there any unfinished business to take care of before we call a new pastor?

1. Why did our former pastor resign?

The answer may be simple. Perhaps his physical ability was declining, or he felt he had stayed long enough and that his work was finished. Maybe he was called to another ministry and it was obvious to everybody that the call was God's will. He may have felt that the leaders were not on the same page with him in their planning, and it was wisest to part company before too much damage was done. (See Acts 15:36–41.) Sadly, the pastor may have been involved in some ministerial indiscretion that demanded a resignation. If the matter was dealt with biblically and help was provided, keep praying for him and his family and give what encouragement you can.

If the pastor's resignation was agreeable to all or most of the church family and seemed to be in God's will, rejoice and move on. This ought to make it easier for the new minister. There's no sense doing a lingering autopsy on a healthy situation. However, if your review causes other factors to emerge, discuss them honestly, pray for wisdom (James 1:5), and try to understand and benefit from them. The people who do surveys tell us that some of the major causes of unhappy ministerial resignations are (not in order of frequency):

- The pastor experienced repeated conflicts with officers and other members, and these conflicts weren't resolved.
- The congregation expected more than the pastor could provide.
- The pastor expected more than the church could perform.
- The pastor and congregation could not agree on a vision for the church.
- The pastor made changes in the church too fast and in too dictatorial a manner.
- The pastor had staff problems he apparently couldn't handle.
- The pastor and church had serious theological differences.
- The pastor, when a candidate, had a hidden agenda (such as doctrinal changes, bringing the church into a different denomination, friends to replace staff members), and the board and church said no.

2. What part did the congregation play in the matter? The leaders?

Some of the causes for a pastor's resignation, including the issue of serious theological differences, can be settled during the candidating interview, if the committee asks the right questions. For example, the interviewee should not go any further in the process until he expresses an agreement with the church's statement of faith. If he can't be trusted here, where can he be trusted? If the previous pastor resigned over serious theological issues, did somebody slip up during the interview process and assume agreement when there was none? Did this oversight give the candidate the impression that the matter wasn't important? We will deal with these matters when we think later about the candidating process, but it's good to mention them now so we can be prepared to ask the right questions. If these questions weren't asked of the former pastor during the interviewing process, perhaps the church must take some of the responsibility for his departure. Whatever you discover as you discuss the matter, profit from it, and don't let the committee or the church make the same mistakes twice.

This is a good place to mention the fact that some congregations don't deserve godly pastors because the church has a reputation for "chewing 'em up and spitting 'em out." Every candidate has the right to ask you for a pastoral history of the church. If that summary reveals that you change pastors every two-and-a-half years, the candidate has the right to ask you why. The usual cause is a coalition of leaders (and families) that pays the bills and runs everything in the church. If they don't like the new minister, they maneuver him out. If one pastor would remain long enough to build some stature and gain congregational support, he could confront the issue, and the problem might be solved. (The church also might be split, but at least there would be one healthy congregation.) But "the establishment" usually sees to it that the pastors who are called are young and inexperienced and unwilling to risk a family fight.

3. Is there any unfinished business to take care of before we call a new pastor?

If your review of the resignation of the former minister indicates that the board or the congregation was remiss in some way, then apologies are in order. If one or more of the officers handled matters in an unchristian way, more apologies are in order. "Why not just let the matter rest?" someone will ask. Because the past is not dead; it is very much alive and has a way of catching up with us, as David discovered when his chaplain, Nathan, stopped for a visit to remind him about a previous offense that needed to be resolved (2 Samuel 12). And how will you respond if a candidate you would like to call asks his predecessor, "What happened?" Will you be embarrassed?

Faith is living without scheming. The church needs to have a good conscience if it is to enjoy God's blessing. It's as important for us to wash the wounds we've caused (Acts 16:33) as it is to ask the Lord to wash away the sins we've committed (Psalm 51:1–7). *Unfinished business, if not attended to honestly, can stand in the way of "new business," because the Lord may hold back His blessing.* "He who conceals his sins does not prosper, but whoever confesses and renounces them finds mercy" (Proverbs 28:13).

Regardless of how a pastor was terminated, at one time he was called by a majority of the church members, and that means that some, if not many, members of the church still love and appreciate him and his family. Walk softly before the Lord and maintain humility and honesty, lest you unwittingly make matters more difficult for the new pastor you want to call.

TAKING THE TEMPERATURE

How would you describe your church's spiritual health? Is the spiritual temperature cold (Matthew 24:10), lukewarm (Revelation 3:16), or burning (Luke 24:32; Romans 12:11; 2 Timothy 1:6)? According to Acts 2, in the weeks that followed "the birthday of the church," the saints in Jerusalem were unified (44–46), magnified (47a), and multiplied (47b). These are the marks of a healthy church. The saints loved the Lord and one another, the neighbors spoke well of them, and the number of believers increased as the church's witness spread. Even after the enemy tried to silence their witness (Acts 4:1–5:11), the church remained loyal to the Lord. We're told in Acts 5:12–14 that the congregation was still unified and magnified, and that their numbers multiplied. In fact, it was a church that people were afraid to join!

Why take time for a spiritual inventory? *Because this is the best way to identify the needs of the church and discover what kind of pastor you really need.*

Occasionally we are asked to help churches find pastoral candidates, and when we ask, "What kind of a pastor do you need?" we receive the usual description of an ideal pastor, a person who does not exist. We try again. "What are the ministries that your church especially needs at this time in its history?" Silence. *They don't know what their church needs, so obviously they wouldn't recognize the right pastor if he did come along!*

No one pastor can do everything. Some are gifted evangelists and personal witnesses, while others excel in Bible teaching, organization and administration, or outreach and missions. Some ministers aren't exceptional in the pulpit, but they love people, spend time with them, and bring the loving pastoral touch that many congregations sorely need. It would be wise to survey the congregation to learn what kind of leader the people feel they need at this time. Listen to what people say and try to get a feel for the kind of shepherd they want for the flock. Of course, your survey will reveal various prejudices and some nonsensical ideas ("His wife must not be musical, and he must not have gone to the Holy Land!"), but if interpreted carefully, the survey will help to point you in the right direction. The Lord of the harvest places His workers where He wants them (Luke 10:2), and the Sovereign Creator puts His stars in just the right places (Revelation 1:16, 20; 2:1; 3:1). As you pray and carefully weigh the suggestions people give you, the Spirit can guide you. The candidate that doesn't excite you may turn out to be the person that God has prepared to move your congregation forward.

PASTORAL PREFERENCE SURVEY

1. How long have you been a member of this church?
   _____

2. Are you praying faithfully for God to guide in the selection of a new pastor? _____

3. How did our former pastor help you and the church the most? _____

4. Where do you think he did the least for you and the church? _____

5. What three qualities would you like to see our new pastor possess, in order of importance to the church and its needs now?
   (1.)_____
   (2.)_____
   (3.)_____

6. Comments you would like to share. (Use other side if necessary.)

A church secretary made a typographical error, and instead of "First Free Church" wrote "Fist Free Church." We hope it wasn't a Freudian slip. And how would you like to attend the "Free for All Baptist Church" or "The Battleground Baptist Church"? (We have seen these names.) The pastoral preference survey can be a tool to build with, a toy to play with, or a weapon to fight with. Pray that the Spirit will guide the people as they respond and as all of you think and pray together. It's easy to call the wrong pastor just to please the wrong people. Let's determine to call the right pastor to please God and His dedicated people.

chapter 3

The Candidate

[He needs] the heart of a lion, the hide of a hippopotamus, the agility of a greyhound, the patience of a donkey, the wisdom of an elephant, the industry of an ant, and as many lives as a cat.

—Edgar D. Jones

[He is] both a soldier and a shepherd. He must nourish, defend and teach; he must have teeth in his mouth, be able to bite and to fight.

—Martin Luther

Like torches, a light to others, a waste and destruction to themselves.

—Richard Hooker

To some people, the word *candidate* carries an aura of competition and even suspicion, probably because of the political overtones of the word. This is unfortunate, so you must not allow such ideas to creep into your work of finding a pastoral candidate. For one thing, there's no competition in the Lord's work, for we are all "God's fellow workers" (1 Corinthians 3:9), each doing his or her own work for God's glory (John 4:34–38). Our English word *candidate* comes from the Latin word *candidates,* which means "to be clothed in white." The men who ran for office in ancient Rome wore white togas, so the word has a noble pedigree. (If you want a spiritual application of this truth, take time to meditate on Ecclesiastes 9:8; Revelation 3:4–5; 6:11; 7:9–14; and 19:14).

As far as the local church is concerned, a candidate is a person a church has taken through a careful screening process and is now seriously considering calling as the minister of the church. While your committee may be in contact with several potential pastors, it's wrong to turn this important process into a "beauty contest." *The church should hear and consider only one candidate at a time.* We know of churches that heard several candidates in a row and then "bargained" with them to see which one would come at the lowest price. Brothers and sisters, such things ought not so to be!

According to Jesus (John 10:1–14), there are three kinds of people you must not consider calling to the pulpit of the church.

- The *stranger* is a true shepherd, called and equipped by God, *but not God's choice for your flock.* The sheep will not follow him because his "voice" simply doesn't reach their hearts and resonate with their spirits. The fact that a minister has done well in one congregation doesn't mean he will automatically bring the blessing with him to your church.
- The *hireling* is a counterfeit shepherd who views ministry as a job involving a minimum of work and a maximum of benefits. He has no concern for the sheep, and when difficulty and danger arise, instead of leading and protecting the sheep, he runs away to an easier assignment. (Check Nehemiah 6:11 and Acts 20:29–32.) He doesn't seek God's will but negotiates a contract to accomplish his own will. To him, ministry is a business proposition and not an opportunity to serve God and His people.
- The *thief,* like the hireling, is a wolf in sheep's clothing that comes only to ravage the flock. Instead of bringing a life-giving

ministry to the people, he steals, kills, and destroys. His goal might be money, power, prestige, a "more important" church, or perhaps a denominational office. In that disguise he has a hidden agenda, and he will use and abuse people to get what he wants. Ezekiel the prophet described well this dangerous kind of shepherd (Ezekiel 34).

What you must be praying for is the true shepherd the Lord has chosen for you. This is a shepherd who will get to know the sheep and be able to call them by name, who lovingly cares for the sheep and willingly sacrifices for them.

At this point, we want to share an important piece of counsel that will save you and your potential candidates a great deal of trouble: Once a minister is in the selection process, keep him and his family informed, and ask them to keep you informed. In this day of almost instant communication, there is no reason to make people wait days and even weeks for information that concerns their future. A dilatory, procrastinating PSC chairperson should be replaced with one who treats others with kindness and respect.

Now let's look at the five stages in the selection process.

1. A NAME IN A FILE.

Once it is known that the current pastor is leaving, the church immediately prays and seeks God's will in appointing the PSC. This process is usually spelled out in the by-laws. The PSC begins to gather the names of potential candidates by contacting people who know about the church and its particular needs. Former pastors might even have suggestions, and pastors in like-minded churches in your fellowship can help here. (Beware lest they promote themselves! In fact, beware of anybody who tells you "God told him" he was to become the next pastor.) The mature believers in your congregation are good sources of contacts, for they often attend Christian conferences and hear other preachers. There may be people in the church who have a good network of friends in high places who can make suggestions. Most Christian schools, especially seminaries, have an office that handles requests for guest speakers or graduates interested in candidating. Occasionally you find a faculty member who wants to move into a pastorate.

A word of caution: Don't begin your search by writing to all the well-known preachers you hear on radio and see on television and whose books are in your church library. Most of them have invested many difficult years establishing their ministries, and it's not likely the Lord wants to move them. One of Victorian England's leading preachers was Joseph Parker at the City Temple in London. He received an invitation to minister at a much smaller church, and he wrote to the committee, "An eagle does not roost in a sparrow's nest." His reply was saturated with ego, but the message was clear.

At the other extreme, don't discount the younger pastor or even the recent seminary graduate. If you have the right person, and if everybody is patient and prayerful, the church can "grow" a minister whom God will use effectively. Charles Haddon Spurgeon was only nineteen years old when the New Park Street Chapel called him, and the congregation prayed and loved their young pastor into a phenomenal ministry that still continues in the volumes of his printed sermons. Even godly Samuel almost made the mistake of disdaining a youth (1 Samuel 16:1–13). Later, the giant Goliath looked at David and made the same mistake and died because of it (1 Samuel 17). Ev-

In contacting and getting to know potential candidates, use every reasonable means of communication before you spend money on travel. This includes the old-fashioned snail mail, e-mail (if he has a personal account he feels comfortable using for correspondence), and conference calls. Each situation will be different, so learn to be flexible.

Okay, I can see you are good at multi-tasking. Check!

ery church wants a forty-year-old pastor with thirty years' experience, but no such person exists. You can trust the Lord to answer the prayer that helped the first church select a leader—"Lord, you know everyone's heart. Show us which of these . . . you have chosen" (Acts 1:24).

Sometimes the Lord does the unusual and brings a new pastor to you rather quickly. If so, be grateful. It's good for the church family when the former pastor leaves one Sunday and the new pastor begins the next Sunday. But in most congregations, it takes time to find just the right shepherd. *Even before you meet a potential candidate, find out all you can about him, his family, and his ministry.* Learn to separate truth from fiction and never listen to religious gossip. People lied about Jesus and Paul, and they will lie about God's servants today. The important thing is the assurance that each name on the list meets the qualifications given in 1 Timothy 3, Titus 1, and other Scriptures. Turn your file into a prayer list and mention each name to the Lord, asking for His providential leading.

It would be helpful if the PSC spent time examining the qualifications listed in 1 Timothy 3 and Titus 1, and you might want the official board (elders and deacons) to join you in this study. The church probably already has definite convictions about standards for measuring a godly pastor, and these standards may be in print, but it won't hurt to review them. It is especially important that you all are on the same page when it comes to 1 Timothy 3:2—"the husband of but one wife." We're not suggesting that you add to your responsibilities by opening up a church-wide discussion on this controversial verse, but there must be agreement among those of you who are leading the church at this critical time.[1] You must also agree on who will secure the information needed from potential candidates

---

1. Good and godly people, including saintly scholars, have conflicting interpretations of this verse, so let's be charitable with those who disagree with us. As Augustine said, "In essentials, unity; in non-essentials, liberty; in all things, charity." Follow the guidelines your church has laid down.

to ascertain whether they meet the requirements. Note that Paul frequently mentions the home and family and that things financial are also included on the list.

2. A VOICE

One of the most sensitive areas of the pastoral search process is introducing a potential candidate to the church family without creating problems for him in his own place of service. It's somewhat easier when you're considering a man who currently is an assistant on a church staff or serving in a parachurch ministry, but the kind of pastor we're all looking for is probably leading a church that doesn't want to let him go. You must exercise caution and be "as shrewd as snakes and as innocent as doves" (Matthew 10:16). The Lord doesn't usually tear down one ministry in order to build up another one.

However, before you start purchasing plane tickets and barnstorming the country to visit churches, consider beginning by listening to recorded messages if they are available. Many local churches record the pastor's messages, and the PSC can privately secure cassette tapes. To be sure, it takes more than a strong pulpit to make a healthy church, but there is no substitute for the solid exposition of the Word of God. As you listen and later discuss, consider these questions:

- Does he explain and apply God's Word in a clear, loving way?
- Does he "set the table" with nourishing food, or just give the recipe?
- Is there evidence that he not only loves to preach but also loves the people to whom he preaches?
- Does the message exalt Christ and tell people how to be saved?
- Does he use correct grammar?
- Does he say it right the first time, or circle around looking for

a place to land? Does he make the best use of his preaching time, or go off on time-wasting detours?

- Do his messages touch the heart and motivate the will, or just instruct the mind? Does your spirit resonate with him?
- Does he preach the gospel clearly and from his heart give an appeal for people to respond to the Spirit's call?

After the members of the PSC have evaluated the recorded sermons, meet and share your observations about the speaker and the messages, keeping in mind that no preacher is always in top form (James 3:1–2). If you agree that you could listen to him week after week, then start praying and strategizing to bring about a face-to-face meeting. If geography and the church budget permit, a small delegation could visit the speaker's church and hear him personally on his own turf. If at that time you would like a private meeting with the pastor, then you must let him know you are coming and see if he is available *and has an interest in talking with you.* For all you know, he may be in the midst of a church situation that would explode if strangers showed up who looked like a pulpit committee. Avoid e-mail and faxes; phone him at home, and allow him to plan the meeting so that it will not create problems.

There are some advantages in actually visiting the church. For one thing, you will see him preach and not just hear him, and pulpit manners and platform behavior are important. You will also participate in a typical service that he probably helped to plan, and this will give you a basis for discussing his views of worship. You are not meeting to get all your questions answered but to get acquainted and to get a gut-level feeling about the preacher. You are seeking to answer two questions: 1. "Is he interested?" and 2. "Do you want to recommend that the PSC pursue the matter further?"

Note: More than one minister has said no during this initial get-acquainted meeting, only to say maybe a few weeks later. Don't slam the door or burn all the bridges. Keep in touch and pray. After all,

Rumor has it, a pastor search committee from another church is looking at our preacher.

you're asking him and his family to take a drastic step into a new situation, and they need time to understand the facts and assimilate the feelings. Put yourself in their place and be patient.

3. A GUEST PREACHER

When a potential candidate feels the Lord may be leading him to consider your invitation and he indicates his interest, your next task is to introduce him to the church and let the members meet him personally and hear him preach. This need not be done at a Sunday morning worship service, although if the "courting" leads to "engagement," this will eventually take place. People know that the pulpit is vacant, and they will naturally suspect that every guest preacher you invite is a candidate, so get used to it. Just don't create unnecessary problems for the guest preacher back home.

Perhaps he could speak at your annual missions conference or at the commemoration of a church anniversary. If the conventional church calendar doesn't offer any opportunities, then simply invite him as a guest preacher and announce it that way. If expense is no problem to your church and distance no problem to your guests, let him bring his wife and family along, provided that he and his wife feel that's the best way to do it. Each situation is different, and the PSC will have to learn to be flexible. It isn't necessary to roll out any red carpets or prepare for a coronation, but do treat your guests as you would want to be treated yourself.

If the guest preacher agrees, the PSC and official board could meet with him and start some preliminary fact-finding. Have printed information about your church ready for him to take home and read, including a list of questions for him and his wife to consider in case there should be another meeting. (More about these questions in the next section.) While the church officers are meeting with the preacher, some of the gracious ladies of the church should be spending time with his wife, perhaps answering her questions about the community—the schools, shopping, and the other matters that especially concern wives, mothers, and children.

There are times when a guest preacher walks into an unfamiliar church sanctuary and immediately feels very much at home. He has a growing feeling that he "belongs," but he keeps it to himself. As the service progresses, he has a conviction that he could minister there and be satisfied, if that's what the Lord wanted for him. On the other hand, there are times when everything seems to go wrong, from the weather to the sound system, and you wonder if your guest speaker would ever want to return. *Don't press for opinions or decisions; give the matter time.* The Lord is in control, and our times are in His hands (Psalm 31:15).

In the days that follow, the PSC should quietly find out how the people responded to the guest preacher. It should also meet to pray and to weigh the positive and negative factors that have emerged. If all systems seem to say go, and the guest preacher hasn't closed the door, then contact him and invite him to return so that he and the PSC can spend time getting better acquainted and considering this possible change of ministry. If he says no, then put his card in a pending file, because you never know how the Lord may work; then move on to the next possible candidate. However, if the preacher feels positive about pursuing the matter further, work out a time to have him return with his wife and family and prepare for the interview.

How he shares this decision with his own church leaders is up to him, but do all you can to help him reduce tension and present your invitation as a challenge to the leadership of both churches. This is an opportunity for both congregations to obey the command that our Lord gives seven times in Revelation 2–3, "He who has an ear, let him hear what the Spirit says to the churches" (Revelation 2:7, 11, 17, 29; 3:6, 13, 22). Note the plural—"churches." God may have a message for the candidate's present church as the Spirit speaks to the seeking church. There is no competition in the work of the Lord, and as churches take steps of faith, they can learn from each other. If a church doesn't want to seek God's will with their pastor, he might be better off in a different place.

4. An Interviewee

This is a key meeting and the best opportunity for the church leaders to get to know the potential candidate and for the candidate and spouse to get to know the church. Of course, before they come to the meeting, the minister and his wife will want to review the facts about the church that you've given them and then list the questions they want to ask. While the focus will undoubtedly be on the minister and his work, his wife must be included and allowed to share in some of the discussion. She is not only a wife and mother, but if you call her husband, she will probably be expected to become an unpaid assistant pastor on the church staff. She is an important part of the team, so don't let her sit on the bench during this get-acquainted time.

Long before the meeting, try to get as much basic information as you can from your potential candidate, as this will save time when the committee meets. This includes biographical information—education, conversion, call to ministry, and ministry experience, which must be more than a list of dates and places. The ministry summary should also explain why ministry changes took place and how the couple evaluated their work. This summary may also help you discover things to ask about and discuss.

Questions that focus only on quantity (How many hospital visits did you make last year?) don't usually tell much. Try to ask questions that penetrate the heart (What tasks in ministry do you feel best about? What tasks irritate you?) and help to reveal values, likes and dislikes, character traits, goals—things that really count. We heard of one pastor who said hello to every patient in the room or ward and counted each hello as a hospital visit. He made thousands of "hospital visits" every year.

The atmosphere of this meeting is important because it involves one of the most important decisions in the life of a congregation and a minister. If the atmosphere is too informal and not controlled by a structured agenda, you may have an enjoyable gathering, but the work won't get done. On the other hand, if the procedure is so professional and formal that it's a combination of an MRI and a third degree at the police station, the meeting will lack the openness and freedom that's really needed to get to the heart of the matter. If you find nothing to laugh about, or if conversation is listless and routine, stop the meeting and seek God's help. Prayer and planning, plus mature chairing of the meeting, will expedite things considerably. *The goal that motivates the meeting is getting to know each other better,* and the three principles that govern the interview process are:

1. You are allowed to ask the candidate any questions you would be willing to answer if he asked them of you.
2. You are not allowed to ask hypothetical questions. Stick to reality, to the facts.
3. You must *listen* to what is said and note what was not said. See James 1:19 and Proverbs 18:13.

Whatever else you may ask, be sure these questions are included:

1. How do you define *ministry*?
2. How do you measure ministry?
3. What is your approach to making changes in a church?
4. What is your style of leadership?
5. Are you goal oriented, or more of a people person, or a combination of both?
6. How would you determine ministry priorities for this church?
7. Arrange the following in order of your own priorities: church, community, denomination, family. Explain why.

I don't know . . . this one's got a few warts
and moles too.

8. Tell us about your personal devotional life and your family devotional time.
9. How do you respond to criticism and conflict in the church family?
10. Do you feel comfortable doing personal counseling?
11. Do you have a favorite preacher? A favorite author? What is it about these people that interests you and helps you the most?
12. How do you relate to ministers outside our denomination (in terms of fellowship)?
13. What new discovery about the Christian life have you made in the past year? About church ministry? About preaching?
14. What conferences or seminars have been most helpful to you?
15. If you were called to this church, what would be your daily and weekly schedule? How do you handle interruptions and emergencies?
16. What New Testament image of the church is most meaningful to you? Why?
17. What are your main interests outside of pastoral ministry?

Be sure to permit the couple to ask you questions that relate to what you've asked them. The interview must be a two-way street or it will lead to a time-wasting dead end in a cul-de-sac. Be sure to tell the truth. The candidate and his wife have come to be informed, not impressed.

Finances must be discussed in a frank and friendly manner, and both the committee and potential candidate must examine their motives. There's a difference between bargaining and honest discussion. When you bargain, somebody wins and somebody loses, and that's a poor way to begin a pastor-church relationship. Honest discussion may involve the give-and-take of negotiation, but the purpose is to reach a happy agreement and not to overpower an adversary. It won't take long to discover whether "love of money" has entered the scene.

It is God's will that His servants be adequately cared for as they faithfully serve the Lord and His flock. The church provides for him and his family so that he may devote his full time to the ministry—*and faithful ministry is hard work* (1 Timothy 5:17–18; 2 Timothy 2:1–7; Acts 20:34–35). Long before the interview, the PSC should carefully review the relevant Scriptures and take them to heart: Deuteronomy 25:4; Luke 10:7; 1 Corinthians 9:1–14; 1 Timothy 5:17–18; 1 Peter 5:1–4. The committee knows what it costs to live comfortably in your community, and you want your pastor and his family to be a testimony to the faithfulness of the Lord and of His people. As you confer, consider your potential pastor's education and experience as well as the size of your church and of the budget, and be as generous as you can. If the church is generous to the Lord in their giving and to their pastor in their providing, God will bless both and work will prosper to His glory.

We know of an unscrupulous officer who wrote unauthorized checks and stole thousands of dollars from his own church. The bonding company didn't cover the whole amount, so the church cut the pastor's salary to help cover the loss. The Lord moved that pastor to serve another congregation, and the church he left behind began to languish. "There is one who scatters, and yet increases all the more, and there is one who withholds what is justly due, and yet it results only in want" (Proverbs 11:24 NASB). The leaders of that church forgot that Luke 6:38 was still in the Bible.

In evaluating the potential candidate, you should remember that it isn't easy to measure either ministers or their ministries, but we must do the best we can, always seeking the wisdom of the Lord. Would you have chosen Jacob or Gideon or Jeremiah? Not all of the apostles were great leaders, yet Jesus chose them, and the Holy Spirit used them. A loving and believing congregation can help bring out the potential buried in a dedicated servant, and the church makes the minister as much as the minister makes the church.

5. A CANDIDATE

If the interview reveals that the match is a good one, and the PSC agrees that the candidate appears to be God's choice for the church, ask him if he is willing to be an official candidate. *It is the candidate, not the PSC, who decides whether the church should vote on a call.* If he or the PSC have any reservations, it's better to wait, pray, and keep the door open than to rush ahead. The PSC must take the pulse of the church family to see if the people feel confident that this is God's shepherd for them at this time. Share with them the information they need to be able to pray, consider, and vote intelligently. Be available to answer questions. Make it possible for the church family to meet the candidate and his family, probably at a special reception after he preaches some Sunday morning.

It's unwise to recommend a candidate unless the PSC is sure a healthy majority will vote to call him. It's also unwise for the PSC to give him false assurance, because congregations are unpredictable, and the Lord is sovereign. Many a "sure thing" prediction has turned into embarrassment. How and when the vote is taken should be spelled out in the church's bylaws. But, no matter how popular the preacher may be with the congregation or how eager they are for him to come, he and his family ultimately make the decision.

6. A CALLED MINISTER

If the church gives the candidate a healthy majority, he must be informed as soon as possible. He may already be convinced that the Lord wants him to accept a call if it comes, in which case you can announce his acceptance to the congregation. The church then moves into the reception mode, which we'll consider in the next chapter.

He may want to give further consideration to the call, but don't leave the matter open-ended. Agree on a deadline and ask if there's anything that requires further discussion. If even then he's still un-

After much prayer and deliberation, I believe the Lord
is not guiding you to seek a call in this church.

decided, this may be God's way of closing the door. It's dangerous to have a shepherd who can't ascertain the will of God, and it's the Lord who puts the servants where He wants them.

However, the time has not been wasted. The PSC, church officers, and congregation have worked together to determine the will of God, *and God has revealed His will to you.* During this demanding process, you have all learned a few things, and the experience will make the next ventures that much easier.

You're ready now to make plans for the joyful reception of your new shepherd.

INTERLUDE

However, before you send out those invitations, let's pause to face the fact that many months may have gone by and you still don't have a viable candidate. It's a general rule that if the PSC hasn't located some good prospects in at least eighteen months, it's time to take inventory and see what's wrong. Taking inventory isn't always a pleasant experience because we may have to face up to some personal failures, but it's a necessary experience if we're to discover and do God's will. The chairperson should call a meeting and open it up for honest observation, discussion, and confession. These questions may help you examine yourselves and the situation.

1. Are we wasting time? Do we go on detours in our meetings? Are we reading too many résumés? Can one person accomplish what we're now asking two or three to do? Are we handling the same pieces of paper too many times? Is there so much routine that we have no time for progress? Are we postponing decisions that must be made now?

2. Have we failed in accountability? Have we forgotten that we're accountable first of all to the Lord and then to each other—the church leadership and the congregation? We will give an accounting to the Lord one day for our stewardship as committee members. Are we trying to please people in the church, or please Jesus Christ, the head of the church?

3. Are we really praying and encouraging prayer? Over the months, it's easy for prayer leaders to get careless and worship leaders to make the Sunday pastoral prayer routine.

4. Is there some obstacle in our own hearts or in the church that's grieving the Lord? Aaron and Miriam criticized Moses, and this sin held back Israel's progress for a week (Numbers 12). Israel was defeated by a small army because of Achan's disobedience (Joshua 7). "One sinner destroys much good" (Ecclesiastes 9:18). No, we shouldn't go on a personal "witch hunt," but perhaps the official board should call a solemn meeting and ask a guest minister to help lead the congregation in examination, confession, and cleansing. When the early church faced great problems or had to make important decisions, they fasted and prayed. We call breakfast committee meetings and eat and talk!

5. Do we really know what we're looking for? Yes, we must aim for the best, but perhaps our ideals are unrealistic and our priorities out of order. No one candidate can do everything. Are we looking for a "super pastor" who doesn't exist?

6. Does the committee need restructuring? Drastic? Yes, but it must be faced honestly and lovingly. Should a "sanctified obstructionist" be replaced with a more cooperative member? Do we need a new chairperson? Should a member be added who can help expedite things?

7. Does anybody have a hidden agenda? Unless all of us are unselfishly working together in openness and honesty, the Lord can't lead and bless.

Don't get discouraged. God is on the throne; wait before Him and trust Him. Better to wait for the right candidate than to rush ahead and call the wrong one. But don't wait too long!

THE PASTORAL SEARCH COMMITTEE — THE FIRST YEAR

The Pastoral Search Committee has arrived.

THE PASTORAL SEARCH COMMITTEE — THE THIRD YEAR

Don't be alarmed. It's only the Pastoral Search Committee.

chapter 5

Celebration and Dedication

Now thank we all our God, with heart and hands and voices,
Who wondrous things has done, in Whom this world rejoices;
Who from our mothers' arms has blessed us on our way
With countless gifts of love, and still is ours today.
—Martin Rinkart

Now to him who is able to do immeasurably more than all
we ask or imagine, according to his power that is at work
within us, to him be glory in the church and in Christ Jesus
throughout all generations, for ever and ever! Amen.
—Ephesians 3:20–21

Small cheer and great welcome make a merry feast.
—William Shakespeare

THE PURPOSES

For several reasons, your new minister should be formally presented to the congregation and officially installed in his office as shepherd of the flock. The first reason is biblical precedent. In the Old Testament, priests and kings were anointed and publicly installed into their offices (Leviticus 8; 2 Samuel 5:1–5; 1 Kings 1:28–53; 1 Chronicles 21–25), and in the New Testament, the apostles publicly laid hands on new church leaders and prayed for them (Acts 6:1–6; 14:23; 1 Timothy 4:14). Ministers should not magnify themselves, but they certainly ought to dignify their office and glorify the Lord in the way they enter that office and use it.

Second, every congregation needs to be reminded that ministry is a serious matter and that their new pastor is God's gift to the church for their blessing (Ephesians 4:11–12). They must respect the office and learn to love and respect the person filling the office. Yes, the church is an organism, a spiritual body, and Jesus Christ is the Head of the body; but if an organism is not organized, it will die. Churches need spiritual leaders.

A third reason for an official installation is to give special thanks to God for His goodness in sending you a shepherd. It should be a service of worship and dedication that honors Jesus Christ, "that great Shepherd of the sheep" (Hebrews 13:20), who works through His servants to mature and equip His people. A church prospers and glorifies God when His chosen leaders obey His will and the people follow them (Hebrews 13:17). It has well been said that Jesus told His disciples, "I will build my church" (Matthew 16:18), not " I will build your church," or "You will build my church." This meeting should be a time for rededication on the part of the church family.

Fourth, the Pastoral Search Committee ought to be recognized and thanked for its work and then officially dismissed. The best way to focus on the future is to give closure to the past and acknowledge the goodness of God and the faithful work of His servants.

Finally, an official service will help introduce your new pastor to the public at large, who certainly ought to be invited. For this reason, it would be wise to schedule the service at a time convenient for people from other churches (or no churches) to attend. This rules out Sunday morning, although there ought to be some kind of special recognition during the new pastor's first service. Sunday afternoon or evening have both proved acceptable, and a reception ought to follow the service so that people can meet the church's new "first family." Choose the day that best suits your new pastor, and give the pastor and his family opportunity to settle in before you turn the spotlight on them.

Must every organization and ministry of the church be recognized and asked to welcome the new pastor? Probably not. This is a time for the church as a whole to express unity. In the weeks ahead, there will be plenty of opportunities for various groups to invite the new pastor and family to a meeting to learn what the group does in the church. Getting acquainted is important, but it can't be done all at one time. Please don't overwhelm the pastor's family with so many invitations that they get worn out just being friendly. The official board should develop the "get acquainted" schedule and see to it that it's followed.

The entire service should be recorded—perhaps videotaped—for the minister and his family and also for the church archives. Merely record the proceedings—don't produce a show!

THE PREPARATION

The official board and the PSC should work together in planning and appointing workers to handle arrangements for the installation service. What you include depends on what the pastor thinks is important and how long you want the service to be. By all means give the family a scrapbook that includes

- a welcoming letter from the official church board, on behalf of the church family, to be read publicly
- letters from people important to the pastor and his family
- letters from church missionaries he has yet to meet
- letters from denominational leaders, if appropriate
- letters from ministerial friends

If appropriate, include letters from former pastors and from key members who have moved away but still keep in touch with the congregation. Occasional humor is acceptable, but be sure it's really humor and not foolishness. Keep the meeting on a high plane.

Contact people well in advance and ask for their letters or e-mail communications. Not all of the letters need to be read publicly, just the ones that would be especially important—or surprising—to the minister and his family. Is there anybody dear to them who could send a brief word of greeting and encouragement on video?

Some churches give the family a significant welcoming gift, something they can have in their home and keep for many years, but not something that will wear out from use. *Long before the meeting, make it known to the members of the church that they are not to give personal gifts to the new pastor, but that one significant gift will represent them all.* Not only would there be duplicate gifts but also inappropriate gifts from well-meaning people. We know of one young couple in their first church that was given a "holy picture" that they kept in hiding. Fortunately, the donor never visited their apartment. It is definitely not polite for people to give the minister a gift and then visit the home to see if their gift is displayed prominently. By giving one significant gift, you might help the family avoid numerous misunderstandings.

THE PROGRAM

This suggested order of service is easily adapted to the style of worship to which the church family is accustomed.

1. Welcome and call to worship—Psalm 100
2. Invocation
3. Hymn of worship, focusing on the transcendence of the Lord
4. Presentation and welcome of the new pastor and family

5. Official dismissal of the Pastoral Search Committee, with thanks (PSC chairperson may want to say a few words.)
6. Comments by the new pastor, followed by a pastoral prayer
7. Hymn of thanksgiving and rejoicing
8. The church and pastor in covenant (see litany following)
9. Sing "Blest Be the Tie That Binds" or other familiar song that expresses church unity.
10. Message from the Word
11. A hymn of consecration
12. Presentation of the church gift to the family
13. Closing remarks and benediction
14. Fellowship time

Of course, if time permits, appropriate special music may be added. If possible, someone that the new pastor loves and holds in high esteem should give the sermon. It need not be a forty-minute exposition, but it must focus on the glory of Christ and the wonder of His church. Those who are asked to make a few remarks should write down what they want to say, keep it to the point, and read it without comment. On formal occasions such as this, reading from a prepared script is not only proper but also expected and very helpful. A meeting does not have to be long for the blessing to be enduring.

We suggest that, under the leadership of the chairperson of the official board, the new pastor and the congregation enter into a re-newal covenant relationship with the Lord, using a litany such as this one. It is always appropriate to write your own litany; this one is only a suggestion.

Leader (addresses pastor): Do you [full name] accept the call of [church name] to serve the Lord as pastor of this congregation?

Pastor: With all my heart, I do.

Leader: Do you this day consecrate yourself afresh to devote all that you are and all that you have to love this congregation, pray for them, minister the Word to them faithfully, care for them, and serve them in the strength that the Lord gives, to the glory of Jesus Christ?

Pastor: With all my heart, my abilities and gifts, my training, and my resources, I do, and my family joins me.

Leader (addresses the congregation): Do you, the congregation known as [name of the church], accept [pastor's name] as the shepherd God has appointed for you?

Congregation: With all our hearts, we do.

Leader: Do you promise the Lord that you will love your pastor, pray for him daily, listen carefully to God's Word and obey it, and, following his leadership, help [name of church] to share the gospel with the lost, to encourage and assist one another, and to minister to this community in the name of Jesus Christ?

Congregation: With all our hearts, our resources, and our spiritual gifts, we do.

Leader (prays): Let us pray. Gracious Father in heaven, You have heard our promises to You and to one another. In our own strength, we cannot fulfill them; but in Your grace and the power of Your Spirit, we can know and accomplish Your will. We ask your rich blessing to be upon our new pastor and his family, [give their names], and upon this congregation as we joyfully receive them into our community, our church family, our homes, and our hearts. We ask this in the name of Jesus Christ our Lord. Amen.

Worship leader: The congregation sings "Blest Be the Tie That Binds" or other appropriate song that expresses church unity.

Immediately after the benediction, the pastor and his family should be escorted to the fellowship hall to greet the people as they come to the reception. The entire family need not be in an official receiving line, because the younger children may want to get something to eat and then find their new friends, but the pastor, his wife, and older children should be at the door and welcome the people. They should also meet any special guests who came for the occasion.

Now that we've securely installed our new pastor, let us sing "Blest Be the Tie That Binds."

chapter 6

Caring and Continuing

Coming together is a beginning.
Keeping together is progress.
Working together is success.

—Henry Ford

If I could solve all the problems myself, I would.
—Thomas Edison, when asked why he had
a team of twenty-one assistants

Blessed is the leader who seeks the best for those he serves.
—Unknown

Weddings are usually joyful and beautiful, but some of the
marriages that start out that way gradually become miserable
and ugly and end in painful divorce. Marriage is something that
must be worked at twenty-four hours a day, because a healthy, happy
relationship doesn't come by chance but by choice. A good marriage
requires a great deal of love, sacrifice, and patience, and what's true
of a healthy marriage is true of a healthy church.

An exciting installation service is no guarantee that the resulting
"marriage" will be a success. We all pray that the pastor, his family,
and the congregation will enjoy a happy and fruitful relationship
for many years, but along with our prayers, we also need to work

together to build a church that is "blessable." A godly pastor and a godly people, working together to glorify the Lord, can build the kind of church that the Lord wants to bless.

With this in mind, let's explore the essentials for a long and healthy relationship between the pastor and the congregation.[1] We have mentioned some of these factors in passing before, but now we'd like to get more specific.

PRAYER

"If the Lord were to take the Holy Spirit out of this world," said A. W. Tozer, "most of what the church is doing would go right on, and nobody would know the difference." What an indictment! The early church had none of the so-called advantages that churches have today—buildings, large budgets, political influence, slick promotion, or an academically trained ministry—but they did have the power of the Spirit *because they prayed.* God transformed ordinary people into extraordinary servants *because they prayed.* The fruitful minister is a man of prayer, and the faithful congregation is made up of people who pray. Each church has a way of coordinating congregational prayer, but there must be organized prayer in the congregation and in the homes, or the Lord cannot bless. When some visitors asked Charles Haddon Spurgeon the secret of his remarkable ministry, he quietly replied, "My people pray for me."

---

1. We realize that not every pastor is supposed to stay in the same church thirty, forty, or fifty years, and some of those who have done so should have stepped out sooner. Spurgeon said that younger men are prone to leave too soon, and older men stay too long. Sometimes the Lord calls a man to accomplish a specific task, and then He moves him on. This is why "What kind of a minister do we need right now?" is such an important question.

DEDICATION AND DETERMINATION

The pastor's attitude must be like Paul's when he wrote to the church of Corinth: "I do not want to see you now and make only a passing visit; I hope to spend some time with you, if the Lord permits (1 Corinthians 16:7). *"I plan to stay until my work is finished"* must be the pastor's affirmation of faith that God brought him to the church and that there is a work for him to do. *If God had wanted everything in the church to remain as it was, He would not have sent you a new leader.* A wise leader doesn't take down the fences until he knows why they were put up in the first place, nor does he feel compelled to prove himself a great leader by changing everything immediately. If he takes that approach, he's only proving that he's a poor leader. Order in the midst of change and change in the midst of order is the approach the mature and diligent leader takes.

Unless there are grossly unbiblical practices in the church that need immediate attention, the wise pastor spends perhaps a year quietly getting acquainted with the people and the program, assessing the total ministry, and making his private list of priorities, which then becomes a personal prayer list. He realizes, too, that effective ministry requires more than authority; he must also earn stature among the people, and that takes time. As he preaches the truth in love and serves the people faithfully, he wins their love and confidence; and the time comes when he can start thinking about making changes.

At the same time, the leadership of the church must be spiritual and discerning and not dig in their heels and announce, "We shall not be moved!" Instead, they will work and pray with their new pastor to assess the effectiveness of the church's ministry and seek to make improvements. Some churches wisely have written in their constitution, "Once each year, the pastoral staff and the official board shall examine the current ministries of the church and make recommendations for changes." Change for the sake of

Of course, as with any church, we've got a few board members who don't seem to be on the same page as the rest of us.

change is only novelty, but change for the sake of improvement is progress.

To return to our marriage metaphor, the woman who gets married determined to do a makeover on her husband the first year and the man who says to himself, "If it doesn't work, I can always get a divorce," will both weaken and then destroy the marriage. Likewise, a new pastor should not accept a congregation's call thinking that he will change things to suit his agenda, and a congregation must not call a pastor with the assumption that the relationship can be easily broken if things don't work out. No hidden agendas, please, and no escape hatches.

PATIENCE

It takes time for a new minister and his congregation to get to know each other. Learning names is one thing; understanding the people who bear those names is quite something else. The human heart and mind are not easy to fathom (Proverbs 20:5), and too often we get our exercise by jumping to conclusions. Sometimes church members experience difficulty because the new pastor reminds them of a minister they once knew and didn't like, and until this infection is admitted and cleansed, the difficulties with the new minister will continue. But it's also true that ministers sometimes maintain their distance from people who remind them of troublemakers they knew in a previous pastorate, and this poison also must be dealt with.

"Man looks at the outward appearance," the Lord told Samuel, "but the Lord looks at the heart" (1 Samuel 16:7). Judging by height and appearance, Samuel had no idea that Jesse's youngest son, David, was destined to be Israel's next king. Only God sees the heart, but that's no excuse for ministers not to do their best to understand the people in the church family. The members of the spiritual body that we categorize as "weak" may turn out to be the most indispensable (1 Corinthians 12:21–22). If a minister stays in a church long enough, he will gradually esteem more highly some of the people he at first thought were not very good Christians.

ADEQUATE PROVISION

The longer the pastor stays in the church and remains faithful, the more his diligence and service should be recognized and rewarded (1 Thessalonians 5:12–13; 1 Timothy 5:17–18). But along with providing for the basic necessities, don't forget the extras that help to show that you care—a book allowance; time away to attend conferences and seminars; an adequate vacation; a protected day off; the privilege of occasionally ministering in other places. Surely you want a preacher in your pulpit that other people would want to hear. As the church increases in size, add to the staff and enlist more faithful volunteers from the congregation. In short, *demonstrate that you are backing up your pastor in God's work by sharing some of the burdens.* Ministers must stick to their priorities (Acts 6:1–7). A sabbatical leave gives the pastor spiritual, physical, and intellectual renewal and helps to equip him for the next years of ministry. By all means, set up a solid retirement plan and make it possible for the pastor to own a house.

LEADERSHIP

"Follow my example, as I follow the example of Christ" was Paul's appeal to the Corinthians, and it applies today (1 Corinthians 11:1). Pastors should be leaders, and their leadership should be respected (1 Thessalonians 5:12–13; Hebrews 13:7, 17). This admonition doesn't rule out discussion or even disagreement, but people can walk together arm-in-arm even if they can't see eye-to-eye. Disagreements are challenges to exercise love and patience, listen to one another, seek the help of God, and search the Scriptures for the Lord's guidance. But once a decision has been made, let everybody get behind

In recognition of your three decades of faithful service to First Church, the board has decided to give you your first afternoon off . . . and we promise not to call you at home.

it and pray and work for success. We recall a church treasurer, a good and godly man, who was unhappy about the church building program and created some problems. After the building was completed, the man had the courage and honesty to go to the pastor and apologize for his attitude and words. But we also recall a pastor who refused to listen to the counsel of the board and pushed the church into a new ministry that turned out to be a disaster. He, too, came with his apologies and was forgiven, and he was a better man for the experience.

Pastors aren't supposed to sing solos and expect everybody to applaud. Their calling is to help the leaders and other members of the church *to sing their own parts in harmony,* with everybody reading off the same page. Uniformity means a pastor is a dictator; diversity with unity means he's a leader. There is such a thing as "Her Majesty's Loyal Opposition," and heeding their warnings could keep you out of a storm (see Acts 27).

We say it again: Everything rises and falls with leadership. Your pastor may not be a gifted administrator, but he must give vision and direction to the church and see to it that gifted people handle the administrative details and that the church stays on target.

BIBLICAL MEASUREMENTS FOR MINISTRY

How do you measure ministry? How can you be sure that the programs of the church are producing authentic disciples of Jesus Christ who, in turn, are influencing others to trust Him? Younger executives on the church board may be prone to see the church as a business, so they measure everything quantitatively. Alas, we know of some fine pastors who were slain by their executive statistical sabers and forced to move elsewhere. Yes, there is a book in the Bible called Numbers, but besides recording statistics, it also gives the account of Israel's great sin that cost Moses and an entire generation entrance into Canaan.

There must be annual reviews and assessments of the people who share in the work of the ministry, beginning with the pastors and elders. Perhaps the pastor's work is the most difficult to evaluate and yet the easiest to criticize. One of the first problems the early church faced was a criticism of the apostles by people who felt neglected (Acts 6:1–4). We suggest that you take 1 Corinthians 3 as a guide. Note that there are three pictures of the church in this chapter and that each picture represents a goal toward which the church must strive.

1. The church is a family, and the goal is maturity (3:1–4).
2. The church is a field, and the goal is quantity (3:5–9a).
3. The church is a temple, and the goal is quality (3:9b–22).

The spiritual family. No family is perfect, including the church family, but without the help of the family, we would not be prepared for adult life. One of the most important ministries of the local church is to help mature and equip the people of God for life and service (Ephesians 4:11–16; Colossians 1:28–29; Hebrews 13:20– 21). Even the problems and disagreements in the family help us learn, grow up, and become more like Christ. That's the big test: Is the church family becoming more like Jesus Christ, and does this maturing reveal itself in the committee meetings, the giving, the volunteering, and the solving of personal problems? Are the new believers learning how to speak, to walk, to stand, and to serve? Are people discovering their gifts, developing them and dedicating them to Christ's service?

As a "spiritual parent" (1 Corinthians 4:14–15), the pastor feeds the family the Word of God (1 Corinthians 3:1–2) and longs to see them grow from a diet of milk to a diet of bread (Matthew 4:4), solid food (Hebrews 5:11–14) and honey (Psalm 19:10; 119:103). As people mature spiritually, they express their love to God in more mature ways, and this brings new depth to the worship services and the prayer meetings. Little children crave entertainment, but maturing people want enrichment and enlightenment.

The field. The goal of the farmer is quantity; he wants to get back far more grain than he planted. Where there is life, there is growth; and while not every church becomes a megachurch, every church ought to bear "fruit . . . more fruit . . . [and] more fruit (John 15:1–5). *God is interested in quantity.* His command to "be fruitful and increase in number"(Genesis 1:22, 28; 8:17; 9:1, 7) applies to the spiritual as well as the natural. To be sure, numbers aren't the only measure of success, for there's a vast difference between building a church and gathering a crowd; but numbers must not be ignored. Charles Spurgeon said that those who criticize statistics usually have none to report, and he was right.

The book of Acts is the record of the numerical and geographical growth of the early church as it was empowered and impelled by the Holy Spirit. God gives each of His children at least one spiritual gift. Each one has a work to do in the field, and there is no competition among the laborers (John 4:34–38). We sow in tears but eventually reap in joy as we bring the sheaves to the Lord of the harvest (Psalm 126), and every worker will receive his or her own reward (1 Corinthians 4:5). The goal of our hard work together in the field is *quantity.* This means more people coming to know the Lord and living for the Lord and serving Him. It means more prayer to the Lord for His help as we plant more churches and as we send out more witnesses to serve the Lord around the world. It means more sacrificial giving to pay the bills so that all of this can be done to bring more glory to the Lord.

The temple. Now we move from quantity to quality, two goals that are friends and not enemies. People who teach that a church must choose between quantity and quality are believing a lie and perhaps using that lie to cover up their own lack of success. People who teach that a church must choose between quantity and quality have been deceived by a false dilemma. They may even take comfort in their

I say . . . who's with me on this? Who's willing to put on the full armor of God and go into spiritual battle with me?

lack of quantity by reminding themselves that they do have quality, believing the two cannot co-exist. Where there is true spiritual quality, there will usually be the blessing of God and the growth that God wants to give. Although the temple metaphor is often applied to Christians individually, the basic interpretation refers to the building of the local church. (The pronouns are plural in verses 16 and 17.)

The gold, silver, and costly stones represent the truth of God as found in the Word of God (Proverbs 2:1–10; 3:13–15; 8:10–21), and this takes us straight to the pulpit, the Sunday school class, the home Bible studies, and wherever in the church program somebody is sharing the Word. In the Corinthian church, the leaders were paying more attention to the wisdom of men than to the Word of God (1 Corinthians 1:17–2:13; 3:19), and this was resulting in pride, disputes, and divisions. Not only your pastor, but all the teachers and leaders in your congregation must mine the Word, find and mint the treasures of truth buried in it, and then make it a part of their own lives and the lives of those to whom they minister. *Every sermon preached, every lesson taught, every program presented and every song sung must be based on biblical truth.* "To the law and to the testimony! If they do not speak according to this word, they have no light of dawn" (Isaiah 8:20).

PROTECTION

According to Paul, there can be enemies *within* the church, even in the leadership, who want to usurp authority and impose their own will on the people; and there are already enemies *outside* the church, trying to get in and take over (Acts 20:28–31). The pastor and elders must constantly guard both themselves and the flock and protect the church from the invasion of unspiritual leaders and the infection of unbiblical doctrines. But at the same time, the elders must protect their shepherd from the attacks of unscrupulous or ignorant professing Christians. Here is what you do:

1. Never listen to any accusation against your preacher or another leader unless two or three witnesses are present (2 Corinthians 13:1; 1 Timothy 5:19–20). This usually stops the false
   accusers at the start. People who have legitimate concerns
   based on real facts will want witnesses present. Accusation
   without witnesses is slander.
2. "[D]o nothing out of favoritism" (1 Timothy 5:21). No matter
   how long the accusers have been in the church, how much they
   give or how many offices they have held, if they are wrong,
   they are wrong, and they must be dealt with biblically.
3. Without compromise, but with much love and prayer, aim
   for a win/win situation in which both the pastor and the accusers learn and grow, but in no way undermine the pastor's
   authority as the leader of the church. "Those who sin are to
   be rebuked publicly, so that the others may take warning"
   (1 Timothy 5:20).

One of the most difficult leadership challenges to deal with is
the opposition of the "church boss" who has "run things" for years
and successfully frightened off several pastors. If your new pastor
is a godly man of discernment, he'll probably detect the problem
during the candidate process and will not be caught by surprise.
When the enemy begins to work, rally around your pastor and see
him through the battle. Our goal is to help everybody obey God and
grow in grace, so be patient and prayerful, but don't wait too long
or the enemy may increase in number and strength. The shepherd is
always protecting the sheep, but sometimes the sheep must protect
the shepherd. No member of the church should tolerate malicious
gossip or a "sanctified obstructionist" who must have his or her own
way. Read 3 John 9–12 and Romans 16:17–20.

AFFIRMATION

A godly pastor doesn't enjoy flattery[2] and will not encourage effusive public praise, both of which sometimes hide enmity and malice. But like all of us, he appreciates sincere affirmation. The lady who told her pastor after the service, "You're getting better!" had a strange way of affirming him, but he understood and thanked her. Publicly recognizing the anniversary of the pastor's installation is one way to let him know he is appreciated, and making the anniversary a special event every five years is recommended. We don't suggest affirmation because preachers are looking for praise or gifts, but because the Bible commands it (1 Thessalonians 5:12–13), and because "the ties that bind" grow stronger whenever people say "thank you" to each other. It's also an opportunity for the pastor to thank the church family and those who have been a special help to him and to the church during the year. This has to be done carefully, but it has been a blessing in many churches.

One of the best affirmations is the official "thank you" that is accompanied by an increase in salary or benefits. This too is biblical (1 Timothy 5:17–18). Also, think about re-decorating the pastor's study and getting some new furnishings, if that meets with his approval.

FORGIVENESS

Real Christians are forgiven and forgiving. We should treat each other the way our Father treats us, and since He forgives us, we forgive each other (Ephesians 4:32). Like everybody else, pastors make mistakes—especially younger pastors just getting started—and some of their ideas will fail, and it's important that we forgive those mistakes and failures and then start over again. (In some churches,

---

2. Flattery is not communication; it is manipulation.

the pastor goes ahead and does what needs to be done and finds it's easier to get forgiveness than permission.)

The freedom to make mistakes and even to fail is a privilege that goes along with love and humility. "Love . . . keeps no record of wrongs" (1 Corinthians 13:6). Forgiveness is an essential ingredient for success in any kind of partnership, especially marriage and ministry. There's no room in an official meeting for the "We-told-you-so" attitude that builds walls instead of bridges and refuses to allow a penitent to wash the wounds. The godly English minister Thomas Fuller said, "He that cannot forgive others breaks the bridge over which he must pass himself; for every man has need to be forgiven." If you want to let the devil establish a beachhead in the church, allow people to cultivate an unforgiving spirit (2 Corinthians 1:5–11).

Back in our seminary days, we heard this little poem:

> To live above, with saints we love,
> Will certainly be glory.
> To live below, with saints we know—
> Well, that's another story.

Alas, sometimes this poem does come true, but not always. It is possible for a pastor and a congregation to invest years in loving the Lord and each other, serving Him joyfully together, growing together, and by this bringing great glory to Jesus Christ. "Be completely humble and gentle; be patient, bearing with one another in love. Make every effort to keep the unity of the Spirit through the bond of peace" (Ephesians 4:2–3). "Make every effort" means "show diligence, be zealous and eager." In other words, put as much eagerness and energy into building and maintaining your Christian relationships as you do improving your golf game or preparing for a vacation trip. "If Mamma ain't happy, nobody's happy," is a popular principle for family life that may be bad grammar, but it's very good counsel. Let's rephrase it: "If the pastor isn't happy, the church won't be a happy fellowship."

Let's rise above the petty things that have brought distress and division to God's people, and let's determine in our hearts to be among those who sing, "How good and pleasant it is when brothers live together in unity!" (Psalm 133:1).

Problems and Benefits
During the Transition

For the past ten years, author Robert Spradling has worked with several churches without pastors. The transition period without pastors may present both problems and benefits. The following is a summary of some of the most common problems and benefits he has observed in his work.

POTENTIAL PROBLEMS FOR
CHURCHES WITHOUT A PASTOR

1. Failure to structure a qualified pastoral search committee.

Without a qualified pastoral search committee, those involved in the process of searching for a pastor may look for the easiest, quickest, and cheapest way.

For example, a pastor in Virginia retired after forty years in the same church. The church quickly called his assistant to be the senior pastor. While the assistant had good "people" skills, he was not a strong leader or gifted preacher, but "everybody liked him." One of the primary reasons for his call was to avoid the cost of moving a new pastor from a distant location. The church stopped growing, and many of the church members who liked him moved to other churches where they liked another pastor better. The leadership of the church hoped that a quick transition of pastors would keep everything in place, but the opposite occurred.

God seeks to bring churches and pastors together, and when He does, His blessing follows (Acts 20:28).

2. The perception of a leadership vacuum.

The belief that there is an opportunity to seize a leadership role may cause some church members to attempt to fill the gap. If the most aggressive, outspoken, and unqualified take over the task of seeking a new pastor, securing the wrong man may be the result. "Church bosses" tend to look for pastors they believe will do their bidding, which may not correspond to the will of God. God may have a different type of leader for different periods in the development of a church. Wise leaders will seek that special person.

3. Lack of communication from the search committee to the congregation.

A measure of confidentiality is required in all contact and correspondence with a potential pastoral candidate. However, when a committee adopts a "we know what is best" attitude, the result may be unrest and mistrust among the congregation. Rumors will circulate throughout the church body, but a regular flow of information will help suppress this tendency. Regular reports—verbal, visual, and written—will help keep the congregation informed of the committee's work.

4. Information overload.

The accumulation of résumés and names of potential candidates can make the paring process a formidable task. Some committee members feel obligated to deal with every résumé and name. The search committee should develop some basic standards that will help eliminate the unqualified.

A church in North Carolina received over one hundred résumés and names in the first few months of their search. A church in Indiana received over two hundred résumés when their pastor resigned. It is ironic that, in God's providential working, the church that received one hundred résumés located their current pastor from an unexpected source. God is not bound to provide according to the structural procedures of the PSC.

5. Intensified activity by the world, the flesh, and the devil.

Satan seems to work overtime when a church is without a shepherd.

A pastor was asked to resign when his adulterous relationship with the church secretary was discovered. For the next year, it seemed that anything that could go wrong, did. Business meetings were tension-filled with loud disagreements and arguments about every matter that came before the congregation. Board members spent a great deal of time in counseling sessions with members of the congregation, helping them deal with issues that seemed to be endless. Church discipline became a necessity when a member of the church was dismissed for unethical and unchristian-like conduct at a business meeting. Despite these and many other difficulties, the "sanctified sanity of the saints" prevailed. The church now believes that both the wait and the warfare strengthened the church in preparation for a new pastor.

POTENTIAL BENEFITS FOR
CHURCHES WITHOUT A PASTOR

1. An interim pastor.

Sometimes an older, retired pastor can be of great assistance while a church looks for a new pastor. His presence, spiritual leadership, and pulpit ministry provide comfort and stability. A large church that was without a pastor for three years was blessed by the work of a veteran minister. The church remained steady until the current pastor was called. It is not unusual for an interim to be an improvement over the previous pastor.

2. An improved atmosphere in the church.

When a pastor leaves a church under a cloud of moral failure or constant conflict, his departure may result in an improved spirit in the church. In one situation where there was conflict between a pastor and the church, the pastor eventually resigned. Even after the first year of being without a pastor, the mood of the congregation continued to be upbeat and optimistic. With joy and anticipation, the congregation welcomed the new pastor to a long and fruitful ministry.

3. A new appreciation for prayer.

Special prayer meetings that seek the Lord's direction for a new pastor bring a sense of dependence on the Lord. A small church scheduled a series of church-wide prayer meetings for the specific purpose of asking the Lord's guidance in calling a new pastor. One of the joys of a new pastor is to hear members of the congregation say, "Pastor, we prayed for you, and we believe you came to our church as an answer to prayer."

4. Leadership that arises from unexpected quarters.

In a church where the pastor has been the dominant leader, sometimes leaders among the congregation remain dormant. When a man who pastored the same church for over thirty years resigned, latent leaders from the congregation were elected to serve on boards and committees. The search committee chairman, along with other qualified members, provided superb leadership during a difficult two-year period. Their dedicated and often unappreciated service culminated in the call of God's man to the church. God always has leaders "for such a time as this" (Esther 4:14).

5. The purging process.

People may leave their church for valid reasons. But when a church is without a pastor, pulling together instead of pulling away is usually the better strategy.

The chairman of a pastoral search committee mentioned that he believed his church had been tested and strengthened through the process of calling a pastor, even though some of the membership had gone to other churches. However, the faithful who remained were drawn closer together and closer to the Lord. He believed the purging process had been necessary for the church to be ready to work with the new pastor.

A Suggested Committee Inventory

It's important that the chairperson and the committee members maintain a godly walk, something they should do even if they were not on the committee. Helping the church family select a new pastor is a very serious matter, and if we are serving on the Pastoral Search Committee, we want to be at our best so we can do our best. This personal inventory can help.

1. Am I truly walking with the Lord, devoting time daily to prayer and meditation in the Scriptures? Can I honestly say I am "remaining in Christ" (John 15:1–7)?
2. Am I praying frequently for the committee, especially our chairperson, and for the elders and other church leaders?
3. Is there anything in my own heart against any person, especially a committee member, an officer of the church, or a member of the church?
4. Have I broken confidence and divulged private committee matters?
5. Is serving on the committee proving to be a burden? Am I getting impatient to see the matter settled quickly?
6. Has the Lord burdened me with an important matter relating to the pastoral search that I haven't shared with the chairman?

Has God spoken to me from the Scriptures about this matter?

7. Do I come to committee meetings with faith and expectancy, or am I bored and critical?

8. Am I in close touch with one or two committee members and perhaps unwittingly developing a "committee clique"?

Frequently Asked Questions

From meeting to meeting, individual committee members may have questions in their own minds that relate to the ministry the committee is appointed to fulfill. These questions should first be shared privately with the chairperson, who can answer the inquirer, and then, if the matter is that important, shared with the entire committee, without revealing who asked the question.

1. I've received an anonymous letter giving some information to share with the committee. What should I do?

If a letter isn't worth signing, it probably isn't worth reading. If it contains accusations against a committee member or a candidate, there must be proof (2 Corinthians 13:1). The chairperson will want to investigate quietly and will probably end up burying the matter without informing the other committee members. To spread the matter, unless there is proof, is to plant the seeds for future problems. Slanderous mail should be destroyed, not filed away.

2. What approach do we use when a candidate has relatives in the church?

Qualified candidates shouldn't be penalized because they have relatives in the church. The committee should discuss the matter with the candidate, keeping in mind that the Bible warns against partiality in making judgments about people (Proverbs 24:23; 28:21; 1 Timothy 5:21). Jesus had two sets of brothers in his disciple band, and King David's brothers served in his army (1 Samuel 22:1–2). The important thing is that nobody play favorites. If God calls the candidate to the church, the matter can be worked out privately. It need not become a great issue.

3. Is it safe to call a candidate just out of seminary?

There's a vast difference between age and maturity, training and experience. Some recent graduates might be wiser to work under another pastor and "learn the ropes," while others have had wider experience and are ready to give leadership. Many schools have introduced internship programs that enable students to study and serve at the same time and gain the practical experience they need. For that matter, the fact that a candidate has had ten years' experience is no guarantee of maturity. It may have been only five years' experience two times! And the fact that candidates haven't had much formal training doesn't mean they are unprepared to serve. Reading a good deal of pastoral biography convinces us that God has different ways of preparing His servants. Academic training is important, but spiritual maturity and experience in using the Word are more important. Your committee chairperson should speak to the proper seminary staff people to determine how they assess the individual.

4. Some people in our congregation have strong opinions about Bible translations. The first thing they will want to know is what version the candidate uses.

Then people are likely to be offended, unless the pastor preaches directly from the Greek and Hebrew, which might offend them even more. If your church has officially selected a version and provided pew Bibles, the candidate should be told to try to conform. We see no biblical basis for making a translation a test of fellowship, or-thodoxy, or service, nor do we see why a small group of people in a church family should be catered to and allowed to have their own way. A godly pastor will know how to handle this matter.

5. We visited a candidate's present church and were upset by the music. It isn't the style we want for our own worship services.

Then talk it over with the candidate. Perhaps he doesn't like the worship style either but wasn't able to make any changes, and per-haps you can learn from each other. However, at a time when you want the church family to unite behind a new shepherd, it's unwise to upset the congregation with a new worship style. We don't bar-gain with candidates. The church may start to hemorrhage if things change too rapidly. Preaching must not be divorced from worship, because preaching is an act of worship. The Lord may want you to consider another candidate.

6. How do we know if a candidate has a "hidden agenda"?

The easiest way to find out is to chat privately with somebody who knows what the candidate did at his present church and former churches. However, if the church does call him and he accepts, it's up to the church board to work with their new shepherd to see that there is order in the midst of change and change in the midst of order. More experienced ministers understand this; younger inex-perienced pastors sometimes learn the hard way. The leaders have the right to protect the congregation from "invasion," but the new pastor has the right to present his ideas and be given a fair hearing.

7. Is it possible for us to overemphasize preaching skills?

Yes, it is. Preaching is important, but it takes more than a dy-
namic pulpit to build a strong church. We have visited fine growing
churches led by pastors of average preaching ability. We have also
been in churches where all the pastor can do is preach, and others
have to compensate for his inability to direct a staff or be a sympa-
thetic shepherd. There are ministers who seem to have everything
they need to get the job done, but they are usually called to larger
churches that want a "pulpit giant" and can afford a staff to assist the
senior minister. "Able to teach" is one of the biblical qualifications
for a pastor (1 Timothy 3:2), and "able to teach" implies able to learn
and able to communicate the truth to others. As long as the weekly
messages are biblical, interesting, and practical, the result of prayerful study—plagiarism is *never* permitted—the church will be nour-
ished. Younger preachers learn to preach by preaching and in time
will discover their "voice" and also mature their skills. Be patient.

8. Why not consider several candidates at one time?

The prophet Samuel came close to taking that approach and was
rebuked for it (1 Samuel 16:1–13). To consider each candidate individually is fair to the candidates and keeps the procedure from becoming a "beauty contest" where the church measures one preacher
against another. Most candidates would never enter into that kind
of a search. Take time to get to know the candidates and to pray for
God's direction. It's better to want what you don't have than to have
what you don't want.

9. Should we consider again a candidate who was rejected by the church or who said no to our call?

More than once the minister of God's choice has turned out to be someone who was not chosen by the church or who did not say yes to the church's original call. God's ways are not our ways, but if we pray and sincerely want His will, He will show it to us. Candidates aren't always right, nor are local congregations, and we learn together. Neither Eli nor Samuel understood God's call at first, but in the end, God's will was done (1 Samuel 3).

It's easier to take a second look at a candidate that didn't feel called to your church, because the committee work has already been done and the candidate already knows some basic things about the church. The candidate and spouse may have searched their hearts and decided they made a mistake. They may hesitate to contact the chairperson of the committee, but if the candidate and the committee are praying, God will bring them together. It may be a humbling process for both, but God exalts the humble.

To approach a candidate already rejected by the church is a bit more difficult because the committee's approach might be misunderstood. The candidate may get the impression that you have run out of candidates and are willing to settle for second best. Of course this isn't the case, so write the letter or prepare your phone call prayerfully and carefully. But before you contact the candidate, the elders must be brought into the discussion and pray with you for God's direction. Some of the church members may wonder if the committee knows what it is doing or if it is trying to get out of its work with a shortcut. All of these possible misunderstandings can be explained, and if the elders and the committee agree, the candidate may be approached a second time.

10. I hear people talking about when the "honeymoon" is over. What do they mean?

This is going to be a long answer to a short question, so fasten your seatbelt.

In a local church, the "honeymoon" is the time between the

installation of the new pastor and the occasion of the first major disagreement between the pastor and the board, the pastor and a church committee, the pastor and an influential church member, or—God forbid—the pastor and the entire congregation. Newlyweds know the honeymoon is over when they have their first serious argument and hurt each other by what they say and do. Of course, loving people can settle these matters and grow in maturity, and that's what should happen in a church.

Pastors like to share "You-can-tell-the-honeymoon-is-over-when" jokes, not because they don't take the problems seriously but because laughter is good medicine and helps them to get a better perspective on the situation. You can tell the honeymoon is over when

- the trustees change all the church locks while you are out of town
- the parking lot sign that read "Reserved for Pastor" now reads "Reserved for Visitors"
- the church board calls for a vote of confidence while you are on vacation
- on Pastor Appreciation Sunday, nobody shows up

In any growing human relationship—husband and wife, parent and child, employer and employee—there are occasions of friction and disagreement that must not be ignored, or the growing will be hindered. In a local church, the most likely signal that the honeymoon is over is *disturbing criticism of the pastor from members of the congregation*. Sometimes the critics shoot at the pastor by attacking the spouse or the children. A godly pastor must have the tender heart of a shepherd and the thick hide of a rhinoceros but at the same time honestly deal with criticism. As we have said earlier in this book, no officer or church member should listen to destructive criticism and gossip without having witnesses to verify what was said (2 Corinthians 13:1; Deuteronomy 19:15).

Such criticism is usually evidenced by statements like, "I'm just not being fed," or "His messages are over my head." Sermons are too long or too short; the preacher speaks too soft or too loud or too fast or too slow; he preaches only evangelism, or there isn't enough evangelism. As for the pastoral duties, the new minister visits too much or too little, is not a good administrator, hasn't increased the attendance or the offerings, is too concerned with the young folks and not enough with the older people, and isn't available when you need him. Criticism in the church is bad enough, but when the critics don't even agree, matters are really difficult.

In almost every church there is a small group of malcontents that criticizes more than it serves, and even though we don't accept their attitudes and actions, we do accept them as believers in the family of God. What they say can be dealt with by prayer, love, and kindness, and trusting the Lord to change their hearts. If matters get worse as lies spread, the church board must step in and deal with the offenders.

However, there is a place in the church for friendly criticism. When Charles Spurgeon was a young pastor, for several months he received a postcard almost weekly from an unknown friend who pointed out grammatical errors and other things that didn't belong in a sermon, and he was thankful for the help. In those early years, Spurgeon sometimes allowed his humor to get out of hand in the pulpit, and one week the card read, "Titus 2:8—"Sound speech that cannot be condemned." This kind of criticism is healthy and helpful.

Another signal that the honeymoon is over is the refusal of the church or the board to support the pastor in decisions that are obviously biblical. A pastor in North Carolina dismissed a staff member for improper conduct, and the board approved the action. But when the matter was presented to the congregation, *the board members refused to support their pastor.* He felt betrayed, and rightly so, and even considered resigning. All he said was, "I guess the honeymoon is over." Diminishing popularity is another signal. "The pastor isn't likeable or a people person," say the critics. Every Sunday must be a great success, and every church year a "winning season." But the church is an army fighting a sinister enemy, not a team counting touchdowns, and the cry "Get rid of the coach" probably won't solve the problems. Leadership skills should not be measured only by popularity or statistics.

Usually during the first year or two of the ministry of a new shepherd, most people are enthusiastic, cooperative, and united; but then a congregation may lose that one ingredient that is essential for spiritual power and progress: *commitment.* Many people would rather give money to pay staff people to do the work that the church members are supposed to do (Ephesians 4:11–13), but that isn't God's way of building His church. When commitment starts to wane, the honeymoon is over, and the people really don't care what their pastor thinks. They will often accept a ministry responsibility for a few months and then tell the pastor to find somebody else.

11. How can we as a committee tell if the candidate we're presenting is viable?

God knows just the kind of shepherd each flock needs and when it needs him, even though you and I might wonder what He is doing. We have seen churches in university towns led from triumph to triumph by Spirit-filled pastors with limited educations who were unmoved by the Ph.D.s in their congregations. Here are some indicators that the church and the candidate are a good match.

Unity. If the committee is united in their gut-level assessment of the candidate and enthusiastic about the potential, you have made a good beginning.

Compatibility. When assessing a candidate, personal and cultural compatibility are essential. A pastor from Ohio was pulpit supply for a church in North Carolina, and after his weekend of ministry, the committee said, "He fits the church like a glove. Look no further—he's the one for us." It was "love at first sight," and the love lasted. Of course, there must be agreement in matters of doctrine, polity, and philosophy of ministry, and these vital matters must be settled before the call is issued.

Character. "He must be a person of unchallengeable morality," wrote J. Oswald Sanders. This includes not only practical holiness but also good manners, good habits, discipline, courtesy, humility, faith, hope and love—"and the greatest of these is love" (1 Corinthians 13:13). Nobody is perfect, but that's no excuse for lacking the basics.

Vision. Old Testament prophets were called "seers" because they could see what others could not see. Pastors are not prophets in that sense, but they must look beyond the boundaries to the horizons. Too often a congregation becomes comfortable with what the church is doing and really doesn't want to be bothered with anything new, so the church becomes a parking lot instead of a launching pad. The pastor must see new opportunities for ministry, new areas of service, and new approaches to the solving of problems. We aren't talking about "cosmetic changes" that only change the surface, but deeper changes that open the way to progress. "The field is the world," said Jesus (Matthew 13:38), and no church should settle for a lesser vision.

A Brief Anthology for Personal Meditation and Group Discussion

During this faith journey, each committee member must be at his or her best spiritually, and the group must "keep in step with the Spirit" (Galatians 5:25). Along with enjoying your own personal devotional time each day, your meditating on these selections will encourage you and give direction as you make important decisions.

PRAYER

Read Luke 18:1–8, the parable of the persistent widow and the unjust judge. Note that this is a parable of *contrasts*. God is not like this judge, for He is concerned about us and our needs and will graciously answer in due time. God's people are not like this widow, for we are God's children and have access to His throne. We are rich in Jesus Christ and have God's promises to claim as we pray. If a selfish judge meets the needs of an abandoned widow, how much more will our living heavenly Father meet the needs of His precious children for whom Jesus died!

"That which is begun in prayerlessness must end in misery and humiliation." —William Taylor

"In whatever a man does without God, he must fail miserably or succeed more miserably." —George MacDonald

"Prayer is a mighty instrument, not for getting man's will done in Heaven, but for getting God's will done on earth." —Robert Law

"O God, to whom the church belongs, thank you for giving me a special task and a special place within it. Help me to think of my office in the church as a special place of honor; help me always to think of it as an opportunity to serve others . . . Keep me humble. Help me to be faithful in my duty." —from *More Prayers for the Plain Man* by William Barclay

"All our efficiency without His sufficiency is only a deficiency." —Vance Havner

WISDOM

"And if . . . any of you does not know how to meet any particular problem he has only to ask God—who gives generously to all men without making them feel guilty—and he may be quite sure that the necessary wisdom will be given him. But he must ask in sincere faith without secret doubts" (James 1:5–6). —*The New Testament in Modern English* by J. B. Phillips

"God never gives us discernment in order that we may criticize, but that we may intercede" —Oswald Chambers

"But the wisdom that comes from heaven is first of all pure; then peace-loving, considerate, submissive, full of mercy and good fruit, impartial and sincere" (James 3:17).

"Peace is not the absence of conflict but the presence of calmness and control in the midst of the conflict." —Anonymous

GUIDANCE

"I will instruct you and teach you in the way you should go; I will counsel you and watch over you" (Psalm 32:8). When it comes to knowing the will of God, we are the pupils and He is the teacher, and our first responsibility is to submit to Him. If we are willing to obey, He is willing to lead (John 7:17). He patiently teaches us, and His loving eye is upon us every moment. If we start to make a false step, He is ready to stop us and then lead us back to the main path. If we aren't sure about the next step, if we patiently wait for His leading, He will show us in due time.

The Lord's eyes are on His children, and our eyes should be on the Lord (Hebrews 12:1–2).

"But the plans of the Lord stand firm forever, the purposes of his heart through all generations" (Psalm 33:11). Never fear knowing or doing God's will, because God's will comes from God's heart and is a personal expression of God's love for us. No matter what problems we face or burdens we carry, if we do the will of God, His love will strengthen and encourage us.

COURAGE

It was in the midst of a terrible storm at sea that the apostle Paul twice said to the passengers and crew, "Keep up your courage" (Acts 27:22, 25). Confidence in times of difficulty is an essential for success. Paul's courage was the result of his faith in the Lord, for God had told him he would bear witness in Rome (v. 24). "Fear can keep you out of danger, but courage can support you in it," said Puritan preacher Thomas Fuller. "Surely God is my salvation; I will trust and not be afraid" (Isaiah 12:2).

PATIENCE

While doing the will of God, there will be disappointments and trials, and we need patience and endurance. "You need to persevere so that when you have done the will of God, you will receive what he has promised" (Hebrews 10:36). Patient endurance enables us to carry the burden until the task is complete. "But the fruit of the Spirit is . . . patience" (Galatians 5:22).

The enemy wants to make us impatient with God's will, knowing that impatience often motivates us to rush ahead and do something stupid. "Do not be like the horse or the mule" (Psalm 32:9). Horses rush ahead and mules stubbornly hold back, and in the life of the Christian, both attitudes are wrong. If we truly have faith in God, we will have the patience to wait, for "faith and patience" go together (Hebrews 6:12). Waiting on the Lord while we are serving Him is the ideal balance for the servants of God. We "renew our strength" as we wait (Isaiah 40:30–31), and God prepares us for what He has prepared for us.

COURTESY

Ephesians 4:32—"Be kind and compassionate to one another"— tells us how to treat others, including those we disagree with; and if we obey, the Lord will bless us. As Christians, we stand together on the Word of God, but we are always open to different ways of doing things, and we are willing to hear another point of view. If we would have a listening ear, we must have a loving heart. Interrupting one another, cultivating an adversarial attitude, and refusing to consider fresh ideas will only grieve the Spirit and make the work of the committee more difficult.

Courteous Christians are able to speak the truth in love (Ephesians 4:15) and to disagree without being disagreeable. We must remember that God blesses people we disagree with (Matthew 5:43–48) and that Christian love means treating others the way the Father treats us. It's folly to win an argument and lose Christian character—and maybe a friend.

HUMOR

"A cheerful heart is good medicine," wrote King Solomon (Proverbs 17:22), and this applies to committee members. He also wrote, "A happy heart makes the face cheerful" (Proverbs 15:13). It's better to greet one another with a smile than with a frown. "But the fruit of the Spirit is love, joy . . . " (Galatians 5:22). We aren't talking about silly or vulgar jokes but about the joy of the Lord, which is a source of great strength (Nehemiah 8:10; Hebrews 12:1–3).

There are things we could complain about and people we could criticize, but the medicine of a merry heart heals those wounds and motivates us to become like Barnabas, "a son of encouragement" (Acts 4:36–37). Do your job joyfully, and your joy will be contagious.

FAITH

We are trusting God when we obey Him no matter how we feel, no matter what our circumstances are, or no matter what the consequences might be. Read Hebrews 11.

"Faith and obedience change the mediocre into the miraculous." —Vance Havner

"It is only when we reach our limits that God has most room to work." —Bob Pierce

"Faith is the vitamin that makes all we take from the Bible digestible and makes us able to receive it and assimilate it. If we do not have faith, we cannot get anything." —A. W. Tozer

"Real true faith is man's weakness leaning on God's strength." —D. L. Moody

FAITHFULNESS

Christians are not called to be successful in the eyes of men but to be faithful in the eyes of God. "Now it is required that those who have been given a trust must prove faithful" (1 Corinthians 4:2). May we all hear Him say, "Well done, good and faithful servant" (Matthew 25:21).

ABOUT THE AUTHORS

Robert K. Spradling is a graduate of Piedmont Bible College, Bob Jones University, and Grace Theological Seminary. He pastored First Baptist Church, Northville, Michigan, for six years and Bible Center Church, Charleston, West Virginia, for twenty-six years. Since 1993, he has been the Director of Church Development Services, an extension ministry of Appalachian Bible College. In this capacity, he has served over three hundred churches in nineteen states and Canada.

Warren W. Wiersbe is a Bible teacher, conference speaker, and author of more than 150 books, including the popular BE series of commentaries on every book of the Bible. Dr. Wiersbe, the former senior pastor of Moody Church in Chicago, served as general director of Back to the Bible for five years. In 2002 he received the Gold Medallion Lifetime Achievement Award from the Evangelical Christian Publishers Association. He and his wife, Betty, have four grown children and reside in Lincoln, Nebraska.